WILDLIFE RESCUE

Sea Otter RESCUE

Written and photographed
by Suzi Eszterhas

Owlkids Books

Table of Contents

A Note from Suzi

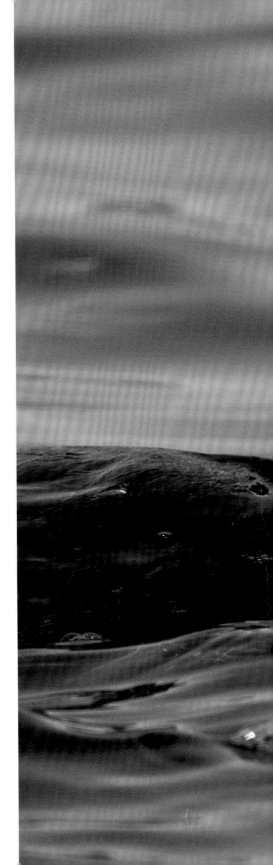

I feel very lucky to have seen sea otters in the wild. As a small child growing up in Northern California, I dreamed of watching these cute and fuzzy animals in the surf. I can still remember when I saw my first sea otter on a school field trip in Monterey. All wrapped up in kelp, floating on its back, the otter was even more adorable than I'd imagined it would be.

But it wasn't until I visited the Alaska SeaLife Center that I saw a sea otter up close. I'll never forget that scared orphaned pup snuggled up in the arms of a Wildlife Rescue Team member. At that moment, I felt so grateful that people care enough about sea otters to rescue them when they need help.

The Alaska SeaLife Center is an amazing place. Many people work there, and each person has a special job and skill set. All the workers have one thing in common—they love marine animals. From microscopic animals that drift in the ocean, to huge, elephant-sized walruses, the Alaska SeaLife Center cares about them all. And when marine mammals in Alaska need to be rescued, team members do an incredible job of saving and helping them.

4

A Place for Marine Mammals

On the shores of Resurrection Bay, in the little town of Seward, Alaska, sits the Alaska SeaLife Center. It is an aquarium visited by people from all over the world. It is also a rescue center for sick and injured ocean animals. Behind the tanks and exhibits, tucked away from the public's view, is a small wildlife hospital. Here the Alaska SeaLife Center's Wildlife Rescue Team treats some special marine mammal patients, including sea lions, seals, walruses, and sea otters.

Tiny orphaned sea otter pups are some of their most adorable patients, and they are definitely the fluffiest! Sea otter pups are also among the hospital's most challenging patients. It takes an entire team of people with different skills, working around the clock, to raise a single otter pup. The Wildlife Rescue Team is made up of veterinarians, biologists, animal care specialists, and highly trained rescuers. The team members went to school for many years and spent a lot of time training in their field. They are all committed to doing everything they can for sea otters.

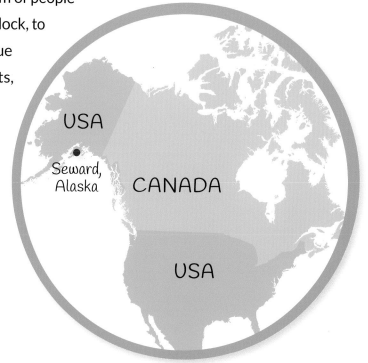

 Like all the members of the rescue team, Animal Care Specialist Julie McCarthy loves her job. What could be more fun than hanging out with sea otters all day?

Studying Sea Otters

Scientists at the Alaska SeaLife Center can learn a lot from studying rescued sea otter pups and adults. Rescued patients give researchers clues about why certain otter populations are decreasing. By examining and treating rescued otters, biologists and researchers can find ways to help sick animals in the wild. They can also see what the otters eat and don't eat, and how a shortage in foods can affect them.

These rescued otters can also help scientists identify pollutants that threaten their species, like pesticides and fertilizers. By studying sick otters, scientists may also see how climate change and ocean temperatures affect them and the foods they eat. Otters teach humans many things, even though we don't speak the same language.

▼ Dr. Carrie Goertz, a veterinarian at the center, looks at a sea otter's blood sample under a microscope. She is checking for disease and parasites.

Orphaned Pups

The Alaska SeaLife Center rescues otters all over the state. Most of the time, the otters are pups that have washed ashore. A pup may be alone, sick, and weak when the team finds it. Often its mother is nowhere in sight. Almost certainly, the pup would die without the rescue team. The team usually doesn't know how a pup has lost its mother. Something could have happened to her. She may have gotten sick and died. Or the mother and pup may have become separated somehow—the mom perhaps caught in a fishing net.

Sea otter moms are devoted mothers, and their pups are completely dependent on them. For the first few weeks of their lives, wild sea otter pups spend much of their time snuggled up on their mother's belly. It is their favorite place to be! Their mothers feed them, keep them dry and warm, protect them from danger, and teach them all the skills they need to survive. The rescuers cannot take the place of an orphaned pup's mom, even though they will take very good care of it. The team's goal is to help the pup grow up healthy and strong.

A sea otter pup's bond with its mom is strong and lasts six months. During this time, a mother teaches her pup everything it needs to know to live in its ocean home.

A Welcome Checkup

After a rescue, the team transports an orphaned pup by plane, boat, or car to the Alaska SeaLife Center. Dr. Carrie Goertz (right), examines the pup when it arrives. This little pup is only three weeks old. It is cold, exhausted, hungry, and very scared. Dr. Goertz makes sure to move slowly and gently as she checks the pup for injuries and illness. With her soft touch, she weighs the pup, takes its temperature, listens to its heartbeat, and tests its blood.

During a pup's entire time at the center, the veterinary staff will keep track of everything it does. They will take notes about what it eats and even how much it poops! Careful records help the team come up with the best plan to keep the pup safe, healthy, and happy. For the next six months, a team member will be with the pup every minute of the day, even when it is asleep.

Time to Eat!

Feeding is the most important part of raising any wild animal, including a sea otter pup. A young orphaned pup must eat every two hours, day and night. It eats a special formula made of milk, pureed clams and squids, water, and vitamins. This blend has some of the same ingredients as its mom's milk. A team member warms the formula so it is the same temperature as a mother sea otter's body.

An otter mother's milk contains special nutrients and vitamins that help keep her pup healthy and safe from disease. Since an orphaned pup has had only small amounts of its mother's milk, it can get sick easily. The first few weeks after a rescue can be a sensitive time for a sea otter pup. The team must make sure the pup eats well, grows, and stays healthy. If the pup drinks plenty of the milk formula while at the center and gains lots of weight, it will have a very good chance of surviving.

Mmm…fishy milk. Sea otter pups always seem to be hungry. The center's formula mimics a sea otter mother's milk, so the pups love it!

Play and Rest

All young pups at the center are kept in the intensive care unit. They sleep, rest, and play in cozy playpens, where they are safe and secure. The playpens are the same kind used for human babies.

In the wild, a sea otter pup would rest on its mom's fuzzy belly, so the team places very soft towels in the pens for the pups to cuddle. A special pad under the towels keeps the pups cool. Since otters live in the cold waters of the Pacific Ocean, it's important to make sure the pups don't get overheated. The temperature needs to be just right.

Sometimes otters rest with their paws over their eyes. Maybe they want to hide their eyes from bright sunlight, or maybe it's just more comfortable that way.

Every baby needs toys—even an orphaned sea otter! The team members carefully select toys that the pup can roll, push, or hold with its small paws. They make sure all toys are safe for chewing, too. Sea otters love to play!

17

Floating Pups

Wild sea otter pups spend most of their time in the water, even before they know how to swim. They are born with a special coat of super-thick fur, or a "float coat," that keeps them from drowning. The float coat is so thick and fluffy that it traps a lot of air between the hairs. It acts like an inflatable life vest to help a pup float. It also keeps a pup warm.

In the wild, a pup spends hours floating while its mother dives for shellfish. To keep her pup from drifting away while she's underwater, a mother often wraps it in kelp, which serves as an anchor. She checks on the pup when she comes up from dives.

At the center, the animal care team makes sure the rescued pup gets plenty of floating time every day. A team member always stands close by, and sometimes reassuringly touches the pup to encourage it to enjoy the water.

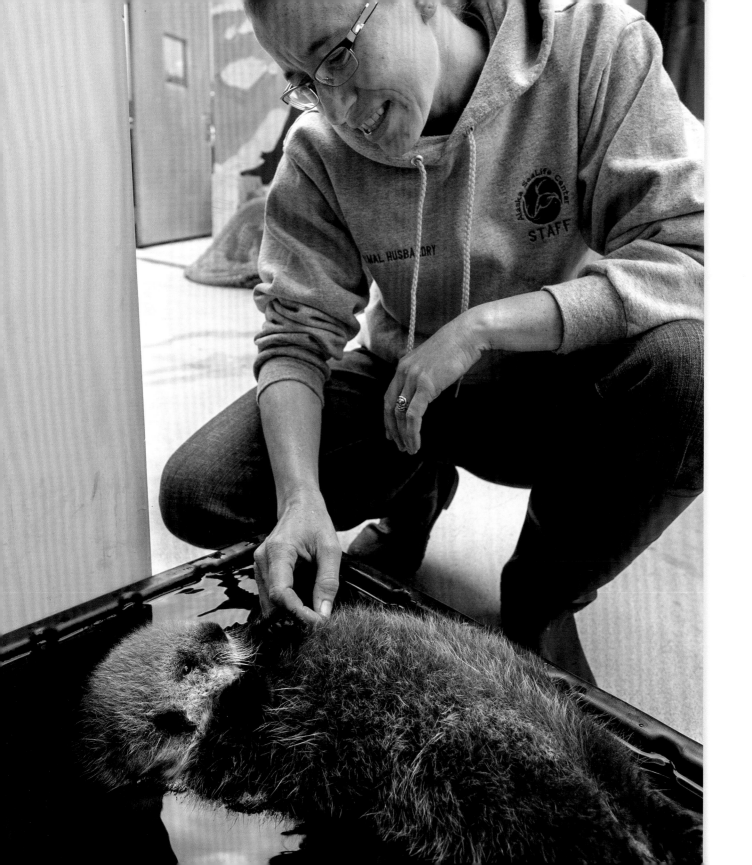

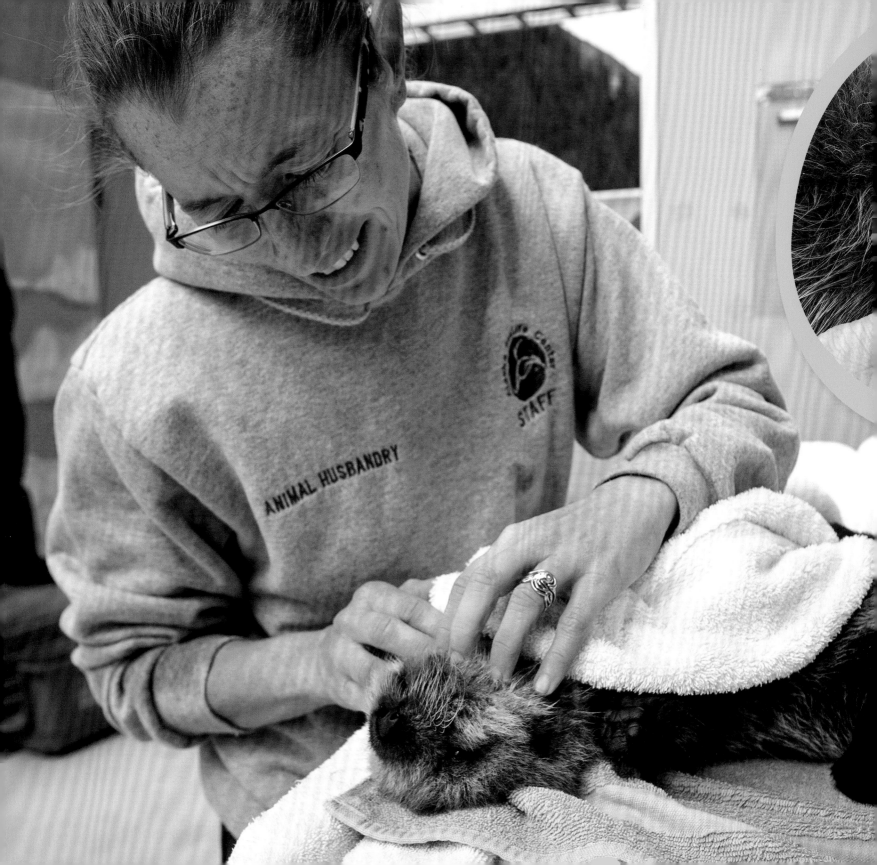

Warm and Dry

Staying warm is an important part of a baby sea otter's life. It is almost as important as eating! Unlike seals and other marine animals, sea otters don't have blubber to keep them warm. Instead, they rely on their dense fur to do the job. It traps body heat next to their skin and blocks out the cold water. Only clean, fluffy fur works, though. Dirty, matted fur can't insulate otters from the cold water.

Otter pups need to be groomed regularly so their fur can do its job. In the wild, otter mothers groom their pups for hours every day. They dry the fur and blow air into the float coat. At the center, the animal care team fills in for the missing mom. When the pup gets wet, a team member carefully and thoroughly dries it off with a towel. Otter pups love to be groomed. Sometimes they squirm with delight because the towels are so cozy and feel so good!

Otter pups need the touch of their mother. This otter holds an animal care specialist's finger for comfort and reassurance.

Icy Fun

In Alaska, otters live in water that is icy for much of the year. They swim through cold, slushy seas, even during winter blizzards. They also spend time hanging out on big chunks of ice. When otters leave the water to rest on land, rocks, or ice, it is called "hauling out." Ice makes a nice cool platform for resting and drying off in the sun.

Ice also makes a great toy for orphaned otter pups at the center. They spend hours batting the ice around with their paws. They love chewing on it, too, which doesn't hurt their teeth. Instead, ice is a yummy, cool treat—just like an ice pop or snow cone is for humans.

At nearly three months, this pup, named Mishka, has outgrown her playpen. She is ready for a larger "big pup" enclosure. Besides her toys, Mishka loves playing with ice cubes.

Pup Talk

Otters are very vocal animals. They make noise to complain when they feel cold and to show when they feel happy. Mothers and pups also call to each other if they become separated. If a pup drifts away while its mother is diving for food, she may have difficulty finding it again in the wavy ocean. The loud calls back and forth help the pair keep track of each other.

At the center, orphaned otters are also very vocal, especially when they want attention. Otters are naturally busy animals that enjoy company. They often want someone to play with. Upon waking up from a nap, this otter calls out for the animal care specialists with a loud, high-pitched squeal. It's playtime!

When this orphaned pup can't see the caretaker over the walls of its enclosure, it calls out loudly.

An animal care specialist answers the urgent call and gently lifts the pup out of the enclosure.

Growing Up

A pup sheds its float coat around the age of three months. It then grows new fur that is more like an adult's, which makes it easier for the pup to dive and swim under water. It's important for the growing pup to practice swimming, diving, and holding its breath. These skills are needed for gathering clams, mussels, and other food under water. Adult sea otters have been known to hold their breath for more than eight minutes!

The team encourages a pup to explore and swim underwater by offering toys that mimic shellfish and rocks. The otter can use them to play a game of diving and retrieving. It helps the pup develop strong muscles, bones, and lungs. It is also a lot of fun! The animal care specialists always stay close by, because the pup is still learning.

After a chilly swim a pup must dry off and get warm. For otters, a big part of growing up is learning how to clean and dry themselves. They squeeze or lick water out of their fur, blow air into it, and roll in the water to trap air between the hairs to fluff them up.

Good grooming can be a matter of life or death for an otter. After months of learning, this orphaned pup has finally got the hang of it and cleans every inch of its body. Looking good!

A Belly Plate

At three months, orphaned pups eat some solid foods, just as they would in the wild. Otters dine on many delicious treats from the sea. The animal care team carefully chops clams, squids, and mussels into tiny pieces and hands them to the pup.

In the wild, an otter's flat belly serves as the perfect dinner plate. To encourage this practice, the animal care team will place some food onto the pup's stomach. In time, the pup will learn to use its belly this way.

Being able to eat solid foods is a big milestone for a healthy, growing pup. It means that the pup will have a greater chance of survival. The animal care team can finally breathe a sigh of relief. This pup will make it!

Weekly Checkups

At least once a week, a veterinarian examines the orphaned pups. The vet checks every pup's coat for shine and smoothness, its mouth for clean teeth and gums, and its eyes for good vision. At certain ages, sea otter pups receive vaccinations to prevent diseases—just like human children do.

As a pup grows older, it becomes more energetic and playful. It also becomes more difficult for the team to handle. The pup thinks the medical instruments are toys and the veterinarian is a playmate. These checkups are important, though, so the staff members are patient. They must make sure a pup is gaining weight and growing bigger each day.

This silly pup has mistaken the tape measure for a toy, and it is making the vet's job a bit difficult.

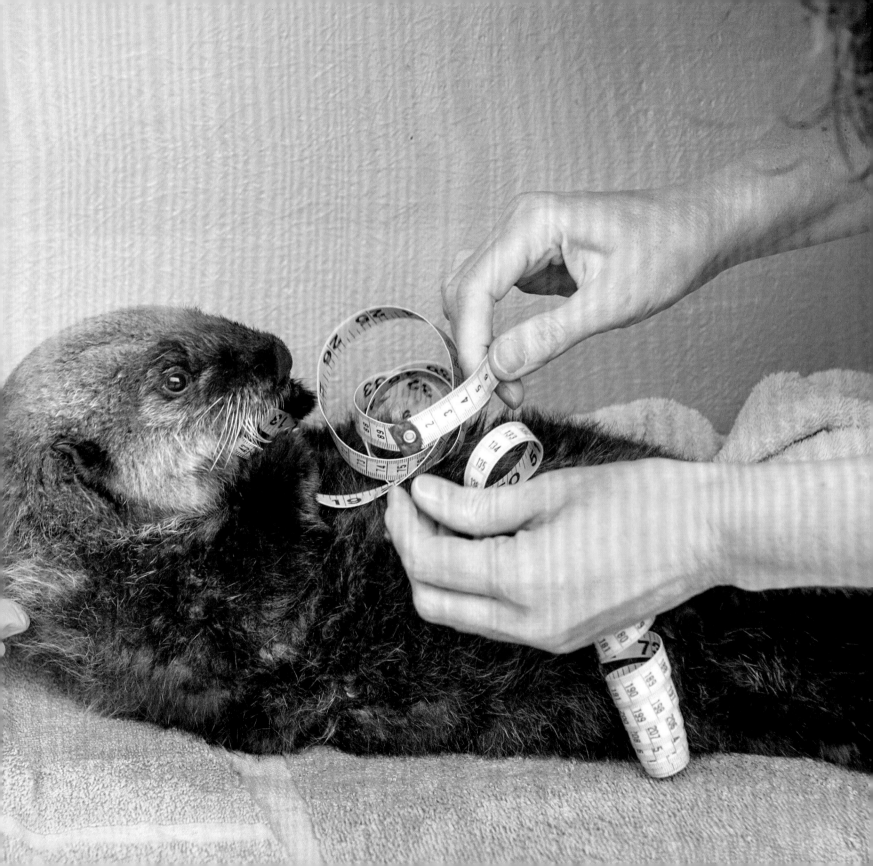

Ready for a Forever Home

At six months, an otter is a juvenile. It is almost adult size. Between six and eighteen months, a juvenile otter in the wild would be ready to leave its mom and find its forever home.

The forever home of a rescued otter depends on how old it was when it arrived at the center. If the otter was older than six months, the team treats its injuries and returns it to the wild as soon as it is healthy. If the otter was rescued as a very young pup, it cannot go back into the wild. The orphaned otter did not get enough quality time with its mother to learn the skills it needs to be on its own. An otter can't learn these skills from humans.

Otters that can't be released to the wild are adopted by other aquariums and zoos, where people will continue to care for them. A team of animal care experts and veterinarians will monitor the otters to ensure they are happy and healthy. These people care deeply about the safety and future of otters.

The Alaska SeaLife Center worked with an artist to make prints of some rescued otters' paws. The otters had fun playing in the paint, and the art was sold to raise funds for the center to help even more otters.

Seattle Aquarium

When orphaned otters arrive at their new forever homes, they can sometimes be a bit shy about meeting the other otters that live there. The shyness goes away quickly, though, and they form fast friendships. Otters are naturally social animals, so the orphaned otters blossom in their new groups. They play, eat, and rest together.

The otters meet new human friends, too. Here, Mishka, the otter pup we met earlier, is getting to know the animal care staff at her new home at the Seattle Aquarium. An important part of the staff's job is to keep Mishka's mind active by teaching her tricks and skills. Otters are intelligent, so playing and learning keeps them happy and healthy.

Mishka gets plenty of her favorite treats, like this yummy crab, at the Seattle Aquarium.

Mishka

SEA OTTER
Female | Born: 2014

Mishka is Russian for "lit...
...an's net, she w...

...entangled
...by the Alas...
...m on Sup...

Visit the Otters

Rescued sea otters that live in zoos and aquariums, like Mishka at the Seattle Aquarium, play an important role in educating people about their species. These otters are visited by millions of people from all over the world. Visitors can laugh at their playful antics and smile at their fluffy faces. They can watch sea otters swim, dive, and eat. At the same time, people can learn about the dangers sea otters face in the wild, such as food shortages and polluted waters.

Many children and adults will never see a sea otter in the wild. Zoos and aquariums make it possible for people to get an up-close view of these amazing creatures. They also help visitors understand why sea otters are threatened and what we can do to help them. Without places like the Alaska SeaLife Center, some of these sea otters would not have survived. By working together, people can help sea otters have a better life and a better future.

Conservation

In the past, people hunted sea otters in order to make coats and hats from their soft, thick fur. By 1911, there were very few sea otters left. Luckily, people around the world decided to ban hunting them. Otter populations have recovered in some areas, but they are still endangered in parts of California and Alaska.

Today, humans threaten sea otters in other ways. When our trash ends up in the ocean, sea otters can get entangled in it or get sick from eating it. Pesticides and fertilizers run off land into the ocean, polluting the sea otters' home and food.

Overfishing also affects sea otters. If fishers take too many shellfish, otters will have little left to eat. Sea otters can also become entangled in fishing nets and drown.

Oil spills can have a big impact on sea otters. When otters come into contact with spilled oil, it flattens their fur. The fur cannot trap air, so it cannot insulate their bodies. Sea otters can quickly become too cold and die.

Rescue workers can save some sea otters, but they can't save the entire species. People must stop polluting the otters' ocean home. Governments and industries need to work to develop alternative energies, such as solar and wind power. This will reduce our use of oil and the risk of oil spills.

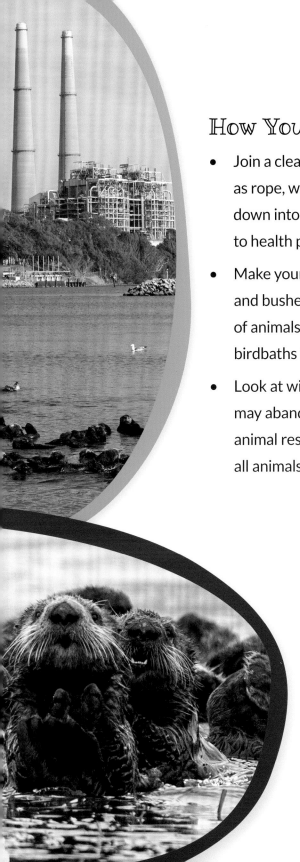

How You Can Help Wildlife

- Join a cleanup group, or start your own stream, river, or coastal cleanup day. Litter such as rope, wire, or plastic rings can entangle animals in the water. Plastic usually breaks down into smaller pieces, which animals may mistake for food. Eating the plastic can lead to health problems and death.

- Make your yard wildlife friendly. Ask your parents if you can plant native plants, trees, and bushes in your yard. These will provide homes and food for many different types of animals, from insects to mammals. Also, consider adding ponds, birdhouses, and birdbaths to your yard.

- Look at wild animals, but do not touch them. Some animals may bite or attack. Others may abandon their young if they think a human has been close by. Tell an adult to call animal rescue if you see an animal that looks injured or sick. Whether wild or domestic, all animals need and deserve our help.

How You Can Help Sea Otters

- Adopt a sea otter at the Alaska SeaLife Center at www.alaskasealife.org.

- Celebrate Sea Otter Awareness Week (the fourth week of September every year). Set up a booth at your school or local mall to teach others about sea otters. Encourage people to write letters to government representatives asking them to help otters.

- Ask your parents to be careful about what goes down the drain. Household chemicals and pet waste are pollutants that are harmful to sea otters and other marine life.

Kids Ask Suzi

1. **Are sea otters really soft?** Yes! They have the softest fur of any animal I have ever felt. Part of what makes their fur so soft is how dense it is. In fact, sea otters have the densest fur of any animal on the planet. They have over 850,000 hairs per square inch (6.5 square centimeters)!

2. **How big are sea otters?** Sea otters are bigger than you'd think. I was amazed the first time I saw an adult up close. They look tiny when you see them surrounded by ocean, but they are really the size of German shepherds. The males can weigh up to 110 pounds (50 kilograms).

3. **Are sea otters smart?** Yes. Sea otters are very intelligent animals. People used to think that apes were the only animals that knew how to use tools, but sea otters can, too. They use small rocks, hard shells, or other objects to pry shellfish from rocks and to hammer them open.

4. **Which animals eat sea otters?** A sea otter's predators are sharks, orcas, bears, and eagles.

5. **What's the coolest thing about sea otters?** Otters have built-in purses, which they use to carry their tools and food. Their purses are extra folds of skin under their armpits.

6. **What do you call a group of sea otters?** A group of sea otters is called a raft. Sea otters are social animals. They like to hang out and rest together in groups. In Alaska, some rafts include more than 1,000 sea otters.

7. **Do sea otters ever come out of the water?** Yes, sea otters sometimes haul out on beaches, rocks, or ice floes. But sea otters are most comfortable in the water. With their webbed hind feet, they appear clumsy and awkward when walking on land.

8. **What is a sea otter's favorite food?** It depends on the otter. In general, sea otters eat clams, mussels, sea urchins, crabs, and abalone. Individual otters tend to prefer a few foods, and this preference is passed on from mother to pup. So if a female eats mostly abalone, her pups will grow up to eat mostly abalone.

Glossary

blubber
A layer of fat beneath the skin of marine mammals such as whales, dolphins, and walruses.

conservation
Protecting animals, plants, and natural resources.

endangered
A word used to describe animal populations or whole species that are in danger of disappearing completely.

float coat
A baby otter's special coat of super-thick fur, which holds air and helps the pup float.

intensive care unit
An area in a hospital where patients receive around-the-clock attention.

kelp
A type of large seaweed.

mammal
Animals that have hair or fur and a backbone. Mammals are warm-blooded. They are born live and drink milk from their mother's body.

microscopic
A word used to describe something so tiny that it can only be seen using a microscope.

pesticide
A poison that is meant to kill insects or other pests.

population
The number of otters living in a certain area.

social
A word that describes animals that live in groups.

Index

Acknowledgments

Dr. Carrie Goertz, Nancy Anderson, Brett Long, Julie McCarthy, Deanna Trogeauga, and Halley Werner of the Alaska SeaLife Center; and Traci Belting of the Seattle Aquarium.

Sources

Traci Belting (curator of mammals and birds at the Seattle Aquarium), in discussion with the author, 2014.

Dr. Carrie Goertz (veterinarian at the Alaska SeaLife Center), in discussion with the author, 2014.

Julie McCarthy (animal care specialist at the Alaska SeaLife Center), in discussion with the author, 2014.

Deanna Trogeauga (aquarist at the Alaska SeaLife Center), in discussion with the author, 2014.

Halley Werner (stranding supervisor at the Alaska SeaLife Center), in discussion with the author, 2014.

Leon, Vicki. *A Raft of Sea Otters*. Montrose, California: London Town Press, 2005.

Seaotters.com (A collaboration of the Monterey Bay Aquarium, U.C. Santa Cruz, U.C. Davis, U.S. Geological Survey, U.S. Fish & Wildlife Service, and the California Department of Fish and Wildlife, among others.)

Owlkids Books acknowledges the financial support of the Canada Council for the Arts, the Ontario Arts Council, the Government of Canada through the Canada Book Fund (CBF) and the Government of Ontario through the Ontario Media Development Corporation's Book Initiative for our publishing activities.

Published in Canada by
Owlkids Books Inc.
10 Lower Spadina Avenue
Toronto, ON M5V 2Z2

Published in the United States by
Owlkids Books Inc.
1700 Fourth Street
Berkeley, CA 94710

Library and Archives Canada Cataloguing in Publication

Eszterhas, Suzi, author
        Sea otter rescue / Suzi Eszterhas.

(Wildlife rescue ; 3)
Includes bibliographical references and index.

ISBN 978-1-77147-175-6 (bound)

        1. Sea otter--Conservation--Alaska--Juvenile literature.
2. Alaska SeaLife Center--Juvenile literature. 3. Wildlife
rescue--Alaska--Juvenile literature. I. Title.

QL737.C25E79 2016   j599.769'509798   C2015-908027-4

Library of Congress Control Number: 2015957721

Edited by: Jessica Burgess and Niki Walker
Designed by: Diane Robertson
Consultant: James Bodkin, Alaska Science Center

Manufactured in Shenzhen, China, in April 2016, by C&C Joint Printing Co.
Job #HP639

A   B   C   D   E   F

Publisher of Chirp, chickaDEE and OWL
www.owlkidsbooks.com | Owlkids Books is a division of